MW00856131

inquire
within

inquire

within

illustrated by mary engelbreit

written by patrick regan

**Andrews McMeel
Publishing**

Kansas City

www.maryengelbreit.com

and Mary Engelbreit are registered trademarks of Mary Engelbreit Enterprises, Inc.

03 04 05 06 07 LPP 10 9 8 7 6 5 4 3 2 1

Design by Stephanie R. Farley and Delsie Chambon

ISBN: 0-7407-3151-3

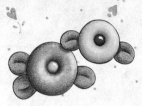

You will recognize
your own path
when you come upon it,
because you will suddenly
have all the energy
and imagination
you will ever need.

— Jerry Gillies

We all face those times
When our confidence fades
And the path of our life
seems unclear.

When worries pile high
   And frustrations build up,
'Til we wish we could
      just disappear.

Perhaps some bad news
Has darkened your door,
Or you're stuck in a rut
you can't see.

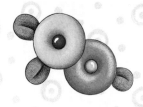

And you're not quite sure how
You got where you are now,
But you know it's not
where you should be.

If you've lost your direction
Or met with rejection,
There's a place you can
search for what's true.

To find all of the answers
to life's tricky questions,
Take some time out
and look into you.

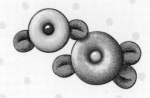

Inside you,
    there's courage . . .

And a deep well of strength
That you likely
    have not ever reached.

There's wisdom
and laughter . . .

and a good deal of beauty
Waiting patiently
to be unleashed.

The trick is to trust
What your heart has
been saying,
And believe that your
instincts are good.

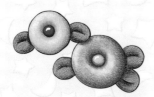

Don't get shook
    by life's rumpus—
  trust your inner compass
To lead yourself
    out of the woods.

The wide, wondrous world
Awaits your contribution
And the gifts you alone
have to give.

PLEASE MAKE A CONTRIBUTION

LIFE

So don't let doubts
delay you
Or worries waylay you,

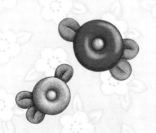

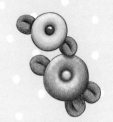

Dive in—
this is your life
to live!

The life you've imagined
 Is yours for the taking
When you make up
 your mind to begin.

And the answers you seek
All reside deep inside.
You need only

inquire

within.